How to Raise 10K in 30 Days:

5 steps to reach your fundraising goal

I0510220

D'ANDRE ASH

DEDICATION

This book is dedicated to Sheree and Isabella.

CONTENTS

Introduction: The habits of the person who wins in fundraising...7

About the Book and the Process...................15

Step 1 Mission Mondays
Clarifying what matters.................................17

Step 2 Team Tuesdays
How to build the right team......................29

Step 3 Why Wednesdays
Crafting a compelling ask............................33

Step 4 Throw a Party Thursdays
Celebrating your cause................................39

Step 5 Follow up Fridays
Systems that turn interest into investment.......51

After the campaign.................................57

Templates...59

About the Author...................................61

It always seems impossible until it's done. - Nelson Mandela.

INTRODUCTION
The habits of the person who wins in fundraising

Successful fundraisers have a track record of generosity. Your previous and current acts of kindness are seeds for your future success. Every gift and gesture you make, small or large, matters. Don't underestimate or undervalue how you've been there for others.

I've heard quite a few people say they want a "nonprofit" without truly understanding what a nonprofit is. It is simply a federal tax designation. Generally, it means that your organization is exempt from certain taxes, depending on your designation. For your contributors, it means that certain contributions to you can be tax-deductible. Some people who have significant income use those deductions to off-set taxes owed at the end of the year. What you may not know is that most folks who start nonprofits do so because they have an abundance of money or profit, and a non-profit is their way to give back or to offset taxes owed from profits made.

What many folks mean when they say they want a nonprofit, is that they have a dream to help a particular people group. But what they don't have is an abundance of cash. That can be a difficult position in which to start and operate a non-profit. Nevertheless, if it is truly your mission, it must be done.

You WILL reach your fundraising goal! If you are reading this book, you probably want to help people. It's likely that you have the background to prove it. That makes you exceptional. But careful. Exceptionality doesn't entitle you (or I) to support. No one owes you a thing. It's the work that we do that earns us credibility. More people are watching you than you know. Everyone that looks at your social media doesn't acknowledge with a "like" or "comment."

Everyone who sees you serving doesn't say, "good job!" But that's no reason to stop. They see you. But you aren't doing it for them. You are doing this because you are called to it. You do it for God, yourself, and the people group you are serving.

Passion

Be sure that you are truly passionate about and connected to your mission. It's helpful to have the ideal logo and a website, but you don't have to have that. Reimagine and rethink what you thought was necessary to raise $10,000. Instead of just great branding and marketing, think integrity, connection, execution, and follow through.

People don't give to causes, they give to people. There is nothing more important than being the type of person that people want to give to. You become that person by being sincere in your passion for your cause, and doing what you said you would do with gifts received. Being solid in this area will contribute to you being viewed as a trustworthy recipient, which moves people to support you and your cause.

You've likely seen tons of advertisements from people who can help you do a myriad of things - but you can easily discern people's sincerity and motives.

Integrity

It's not difficult to find stories of people who have gained public trust only to ruin it by making self-centered decisions. Stay focused on your objectives to raise funds, help others, and execute your plans.

Confidence

Confidence comes from clarity and consistency. I recognize that many of my readers won't have the network that makes raising money easy. But there is an endless source of support that is available to you. Your mission is important enough that previous donors will give again and new major donors will take notice.

Working Steps 1 and 3 of this book will give you the clarity that you need to beam with confidence. When you become confident, the asking becomes the easy part. Asking shifts from an awkward source of anxiety, to a joyful invitation to be a part of something wonderful.

Winning begets confidence. When you implement the steps in this book and reach your goal, you will have created a new sense of unstoppable confidence and momentum and you can go on to duplicate this process or set higher goals.

Consistency

Be consistent in engaging and implementing the strategies offered in this book. And be consistent in your deliverables. Most people quit before they've built the equity that's needed to attract donors. But the truth is that it's only over time that you will prove to yourself and to others that you are worthy of support. Your clarity and consistency in your initiative will grow as you work through the 5 steps and you will grow in confidence.

Generosity

Successful fundraisers have a track record of generosity. Your previous and current acts of kindness are seeds for your future success. Every gift and gesture you make, small or large, matters. Don't underestimate or undervalue how you've been there for others. Something as small as wishing people well on birthdays and special occasions can speak volumes. Don't let special days in peoples' lives go by without at least acknowledging and wishing them well. Not from a manipulative place, but from an overflow joy - truly being able to celebrate with others in their good moments.

If you don't have a track record of generosity, start now. Take a small amount of money and spread it over 5-10 causes that people in your proximity are promoting. Purchase something from the businesses of people close to you and people you admire. Give to fundraising efforts. Your generosity is a seed. This is the new model you must take on and live with.

I am connected to several organizations and people as a donor. Not because I hope to have their particular support, but because I've cultivated a heart of generosity within myself. And I know the fruit of that support will be that supportive people will be attracted to me. On a practical level, it helps me respect the intentionality that is required from people who choose to support me. I then don't take for granted any gift that's given to me or to an organization that I represent. Because I know and respect the intentionality of donors, I don't shirk on the important step of saying thank you in a grand way for every gift. Acknowledging the generosity of others and saying thank you is an important step that we will look at in depth in Step 5.

Use what you have to show up for others. People that you ask to serve or give will have very good reasons not to. They have busy schedules - family obligations, professional responsibilities, previously scheduled appointments, etc. And if they do have time and money to spare, it is theirs to allocate as they choose. It's important to understand what you are asking for when you ask. You must consistently model a willingness to show up, serve, and give to others. You have all of the obligations I listed earlier. And you have the challenge of getting this vision off of the ground. Still you must model the behavior that you expect to see from others. You must show up for people. You must give.

A Sense of Urgency

The best fundraisers that I've met have a sense of urgency. They are action oriented and would rather do something than do nothing. That urgency may be a result of their natural bent, or it may be motivated by a tragedy that has occurred in their life or in the lives of people they care for. Some are motivated by injustices and they can no longer continue to stand on the sidelines and watch as people suffer. Still, for others, they sense a divine "call" to serve a particular population and they can no longer ignore it. In every case, the cause is too important not to act now - even if circumstances aren't perfect. What you may come to understand is that the perfect time is now. That's when opportunities and support

About the Book and the Process

...capital campaigns can be in the planning stages for months or years, ...this process was produced within an entirely different narrative.

Major nonprofits have margin in time and resources. Their capital campaigns can be in the planning stages for months or years, with the campaign stretching for many more years. As you will learn from some of the stories and examples in this book, this process was produced within an entirely different narrative.

The concepts in this book are meant to be put to use without delay to implement a micro-campaign. This method is based off of a proven process that I've navigated successfully dozens of times. I've coined the method as Monday, Tuesday, Wednesday, Thursday,

Friday - with each day representing a step in the process:

Monday - Mission
Tuesday - Team
Wednesday - Why
Thursday - Throwing a party
Friday - Follow up

This process was developed to be executed within 30 days. You'll have an opportunity to determine the amount you need. However, I've specified 10K as a standard target amount. Why $10,000? It's a ground up number. It's a large enough sum to establish something, deliver on programming, and energize business relationships. Most folks on the ground level can visualize how $10,000 would help them make an amazing impact.

This book is designed to jump start your fundraising. Most people don't have a problem dreaming. The problem is in the execution. You will learn much more in this process than you anticipate. You'll learn about your strengths and weaknesses- personally and organizationally.

Step 1
MISSION MONDAY
clarifying what matters

...you don't want sympathy. You want intentional, sustained support. You want people to truly be partners with you in the work - to feel as if your success is theirs.

*I*t all comes down to a transaction. Your hope is that a number of people would fill an envelope, remit an online gift, or give in some form. You probably have two or three people who will give a small gift, today, because they know you. There are others who will give out of obligation. None of those are bad motives - each will move you closer to your goal. It's not hard to get a few sympathy gifts from folks who don't mind giving to charity. But you don't want sympathy. You want intentional, sustained support. You want people to truly be partners with you in the work - to feel as if your success is their success.

In order to turn onlookers into partners, you need to be able to clearly articulate what you do, why you do it, the results you've had, and the results you will create. You need this for your own sense of empowerment and for the critical task of communicating it to the public.

You must have a compelling reason for others to support. You may have heard it said that, "People don't give to need, they give to vision." That's only partially true. People who see themselves as partners will give to needs if you have a track record of results.

To effectively establish and communicate a clear mission, answer these questions:

- What do you do?
- Why do you do it?
- What results have you produced?
- What will support enable you to accomplish?

What do you do?

A person or organization that has not thoughtfully crafted their mission, has not likely organized their work in an efficient way. If the organization does not lean into its mission, it won't accomplish what it set out to do. It's important because it can be a sign post and rally point for you, your team, and for the public. The best mission statements are simple and concise. No one reads a mission statement that's a paragraph long.

Crafting your mission statement is a good opportunity to slow down and think about your work. If done correctly, this is an energizing exercise. A good way to shape your mission statement is to think about two things: who you serve; and how you serve them. Consider if your work is programmatic, event based, relief based, capacity building, etc. Describe the work.
Language matters. Use language that's precise, authentic to your work and that resonates with those who hear or read it.

Emphasize the *"who."* Avoid generalities. When answering this question your accuracy in pinpointing the people group you serve will help signal those who will partner. The right words will capture the interest of people who care about your cause.

Sometimes it's important to use statistics (be sure they are accurate). Certain readers need to see evidence-based data. Include the detrimental implications of your mission not being fulfilled.

Why do you do it?

There is an important motivation, that likely, you rarely discuss. You may not have given it thought or articulation. But in discovering this motivation you will gain fuel for your mission. You'll uncover an energy that will be palpable. It'll attract people to you and your work. They'll feel "connected."

You discover your "why" by quieting yourself and reflecting on what brought you to the point of action. It may have been a long journey or a seminal moment. But there is something that pushed you. Unearth it and share it often with your team and with potential donors.

What results have you produced?

It may be that you are just starting organizationally. But even so, there are probably ways that you have personally done work in this area. Perhaps you haven't opened your clothing closet yet, but you've shared the clothes you have. What direct impact did you make? Share what you've done and how it's impacted people. If you have impacted lots of people, tell the story. If you've only impacted a few, share how significant that impact was.

What will support enable you to accomplish?

What direct impact will you make with the support you are requesting? What practical leaps will your organization make because you've reached your goals?

Example 1 is based off of the formation and actual history of Ash Academy. Example 2 is fictitious. After reading both, fill in the worksheet with your original ideas.

Example 1. Worksheet for Mission Mondays

ASH ACADEMY

What do you do?

We center students who've been ignored. Certain students in our neighborhood aren't achieving their academic potential and we are changing that. We open the doors at 7am with a "before school" program where we serve breakfast and look over homework. Teachers use an innovative online curriculum. We supplement learning with practical life lessons and character development. We care about our students. We have an "after school" program where we offer a meal, homework help and lots of fun.

Why do you do it?

I was at work. Around 10am, I remembered that I left my lunch in the car. While walking to my car, I noticed three boys that appeared to be middle school age running along the property line. Moments later a law enforcement officer swooped onto the parking lot. Her window was down, so I asked if all was well. She told me that the boys had left the nearby highschool and were noticed trespassing on properties nearby. I immediately thought of my troublesome middle school years. I knew that if they were in *my* school, they would be running to school instead of away. The next year, the doors of Ash Academy were open.

What results have you produced?

Last year, we took in a kid who was expelled from his public school. But to us, it wasn't a risk. We were confident that with our environment, and the support of his family, he would do well. He did. We nourished his gifts of storytelling, singing, dancing, and musical talent. He had only one minor infraction that was handled with a restorative framework. Our families are happy with the holistic experience that their students receive.

What will support enable you to accomplish?

A successful campaign means that we will purchase the property next door and expand our capacity to serve 50 more students.

Example 2. Worksheet for Mission Mondays

RHONDA'S SHOW

What do you do?

We style hair for women before job interviews. Our clients are either homeless, in domestic violence shelters, halfway houses, or simply can't afford to visit a salon. We have relationships with women's support facilities in Atlanta that we work with. They reach out to us and our clients come in on the day of or before their interviews. Sometimes, we take the salon to them.

Why do you do it?

I am a hair stylist and I am a single parent. I practice self-care, but much of my time is devoted to working and caring for my children. 3 years ago, a client came in who appeared to be one of the most confident and courageous women I'd met. She had the whole salon laughing the entire time. She later confided in me that she was rebuilt her life after escaping domestic violence. She was doing well for herself. She and I decided to start helping women build their confidence before job interviews by getting their hair styled.

What results have you produced?

For the past 12 months, we've serviced about 4 women every single week. Over 200 total.

What will support enable you to accomplish?

A successful campaign means that we will grow from serving 200 a year to 200 women a month.

Mission Mondays Worksheet

- Q1 What do you do?
- Q2 Why do you do it?
- Q3 What results have you produced?
- Q4 What will support enable you to do?

Q1	Q2
Q4	Q3

Completing this exercise means that you can now clearly communicate your what, your why, your outcomes, and your vision both on paper and in conversation. Remember, it all comes down to transactions. You determine the buy-in of potential supporters. In Step 3, you will use this worksheet to craft and deliver a compelling partnership invitation.

Step 2
TEAM TUESDAY
how to build the right team

People have busy lives, and if you expect them to stop what they are doing to help you, then you better be doing something extraordinary and working hard while you're doing it.

A good measure of your potential to raise funds is your capacity to enlist a core team. There is no magic number, but you need at least 5. When you are sure about your vision, you don't mind evangelizing. In fact, you become magnetic.

I've heard the saying, "If your car breaks down and you stand next to it and wave for help, you'll be waving for a while. But If you start pushing, people will rush to help." It's true for your mission. Social media blasts don't equate to dollars or volunteer support. But if people see you moving, doing something - pushing on something that you could never move on your own, they'll help.

People have busy lives, and if you expect them to stop what they are doing, to help you, then you better be doing something extraordinary and working hard while you're doing it.

This team is only for the campaign. It is not a long-term commitment. You may be connected to or have established a 501c3. Your team may consist of board members, depending on your organizational makeup, or staff. You may be starting from scratch with just an idea. Startups are exciting and have a natural momentum. If this is to fund your start, that's a good place to be, too.

Who should you ask?

those you have helped/supported
mentors

family members that believe in you
peers
friends

What do you need to ask the team to do?

You have one major ask of your team: Deliver an
effective event that:

celebrates and publishes the mission
highlights the work
collects data
invites partnership
raises money

Some particular areas that you can sort out with
your team are:

logistics
sign-in/data capture
donation station
mc
host(s)
audio visual
emails (strategy)
calls
event planning

social media
website
forms

How do you ask?

Directly (see Sample Forms).

Step 3
WHY WEDNESDAY
crafting a compelling ask

You overcome the fear by believing in the value of your work, the worthiness of your constituency, and the likelihood that people will respond positively.

One of the hardest things for professionals to do is ask for money. It can be anxiety provoking. We fret over hearing no. More vivid is the concern about how people will view us for asking. You overcome the fear by believing in the value of your work, the worthiness of your constituency, and the likelihood that people will respond positively. The next few pages will teach you how to ask. We will shape a compelling invitation that's hard to say no to.

You've spent time writing out the answers in the mission worksheet. The next step is to narrow what you have written. Narrow your answers to concise one sentence statements.

- Q1 What do you do?
- Q2 Why do you do it?
- Q3 What results have you produced?
- Q4 What will support enable you to do?

Ex. 1 Ash Academy

Q1 Ash Academy educates marginalized male youth.	Q2 I was once Jay.
Q4 Your gift will make room for 50 more or us.	Q3 J., a gifted musician and singer, was expelled in the 6th grade for a bad decision. He excelled at Ash Academy.

Now to answer what is perhaps the most important question in this book: **Q5: Why should someone give?** Consider the implications of your organization not fulfilling its mission.

Let's put the entire statement together. **Q1, Q2, Q3, Q4 and Q5.** The answers can be ordered in a way that resonates with you.

Example

Q1 Ash Academy educates marginalized male students

Q3 J., a gifted musician and singer, was expelled in the 6th grade for a bad decision. He excelled at Ash Academy.

Q2 I was J.

Q5 Because one decision shouldn't cost a kid everything.

Q4 Your gift will make room for 50 more or us.

Final invitation: Ash Academy educates marginalized male students. J., a gifted musician and singer, was expelled in the 6th grade for a bad decision. He excelled at Ash Academy. I was once J. and we believe one decision shouldn't cost a kid everything. Your gift will make room for 50 more or us.

Example 2 Rhonda's Show

Q1	Q2
Give under-resourced women confidence for job interviews through by styling their hair.	They are mothers, daughters, and future leaders. And we care.
Q4 With your gift we will help 200 a month.	**Q3** We helped 200 last year.

Q5: Why should someone give? **Our clients deserve to feel confident.**

Example

Q1 Give under-resourced women confidence for job interviews through by styling their hair.

Q2 They are mothers, daughters, and future leaders. And we care.

Q5 Our clients deserve to feel confident.

Q3 We helped 200 last year.

Q4 With your gift we will help 200 a month.

Final invitation: We give under-resourced women confidence for job interviews by styling their hair. They are mothers, daughters, and future leaders. We care because our clients deserve to feel confident. Last year, we helped 200. With your gift we will help 200 a month.

Your draft from chapter 1:

Q1 What?	Q2 Why?
Q4 Vision?	**Q3 Results?**

Shortened, one line form:

Q1 What?	Q2 Why?
Q4 Vision?	**Q3 Results?**

Q5. Why should someone give?

Compelling Invitation (Q1-Q5):

Step 4
THROW A PARTY THURSDAY
celebrating your cause

Inexperienced fundraisers bet on a big celebrity gift that brings resources and notoriety in one fell swoop.

A few years back, I met with a person who wanted to share a big idea for fundraising at the school that I founded. As we were walking to my office, they couldn't wait to share the big idea: "You should reach out to Tyler Perry!" They continued, "You can write a letter. Then schedule a tour and talk to him while you are there?" I asked, "Do you have a contact?" They replied, "No, but you can send an email or go up to the security gate and go from there." I'm sure that I couldn't mask my lack of enthusiasm for the idea. And I didn't miss that they had a suggestion for me to follow through on, but never volunteered their time. Nevertheless, I accommodated the conversation for 3-5 minutes and thanked them for the suggestion. If I had $100 for every time that's been suggested to me, I'd never have to raise funds again.

The title of this chapter is not Tyler Perry Thursdays. That's because it's unlikely that Tyler Perry, nor any other celebrity will provide the "big donation" that you desire. At least not yet.

I'm confident in suggesting that may not be what you need at this stage. Inexperienced fundraisers bet on a big celebrity gift that brings resources and notoriety in one fell swoop. The truth is that without relationship, that type of gift rarely happens. And by relationship, I don't mean you actually knowing a celebrity.

It could be that your previous work has impacted someone who has influence with a power broker that's concerned about your cause. Relationship could also mean something entirely different.

As I said in the introduction, there are people watching you that you are not aware of. They see your consistency and feel connected to you and your work. That is, if you've been consistent in your work.

Everything is relationship building and donor cultivation. Every touch matters. What you do today is either building or neglecting relationships with potential donors.The event that you produce will build relationships and simultaneously build your donor base. We will cover the event and the marketing.

The Event

In 2012, I contracted with a school as chaplain and community liaison. One of the tasks that I took on was fundraising. We decided to participate in Giving Tuesday, which is a nationwide day of giving on the Tuesday after Thanksgiving. Funds raised would upgrade computers in the technology center. The challenge was that it was a little over 30 days out.

The principal had participated in Giving Tuesday, before and raised a little over $1,000. She advised that we set a goal at $5,000 and to consider it a success if we reached $2,000. I suggested that we will raise the goal to $10,000. She reluctantly agreed to set $10,000 as our public goal, while internally her expectation was still at $2,000.

At the next staff meeting, we shared with the teachers that we would coordinate a fundraising event and what we would do with the proceeds. They were ecstatic. They began to email me (during the later portions of the meeting) great ideas and offer their support.

We soon shaped a "curriculum night." There would be stations throughout the gymnasium where teachers and students would set up stations to highlight the projects that classrooms we were working on. Every 10 minutes, a different class would get on stage and present in a way that would highlight the talents of that class and share what they had learned.

On curriculum night there was a joyful and celebratory mood. Teachers had been advertising the event, and we had even raised $1,200 before the event began. The principal was the MC. She repeatedly shared our purpose, goal for the evening, and instructed people on how they could give at donation stations and online. As the evening progressed, the most critical suggestion she gave was this: "Thank you for being here. If you know some who couldn't make it, or someone who cares about our school and our students, text them. Let them know that we are at ___% of our goal and invite them to give. Post where you are on social media and ask friends to give online or make a pledge."

That simple request took us from just under $4,000 to slightly over $6,000! When we updated the tracker, the crowd went wild! That momentum excited the crowd and they boosted us to $7,100. Ten minutes before the close of the event, a staff person got a phone call from a person who wanted to remain anonymous. They gave a $4,000 gift! We closed the campaign with over $11,000!

Your event doesn't have to be a banquet (unless a banquet is culturally relevant or has been effective for you or in the past), but it should be a celebration, and a "party-like environment!"

Build your event based on a few questions: What successes should you celebrate? What resources do you have? What's considered "on brand" for you?

What successes should you celebrate?

Within the past year, there have been at least a few occurrences that you wish the world could know about - things that distinguish your work from others. Perhaps there is a person that you've helped that most exemplifies the impact that you seek to make. That's what needs to be centered at your event. People support people. Tell the stories that will move your audience to act.

What resources do you have?

Whatever you do, it doesn't have to be expensive or extravagant. Use the resources and connections that you have. If you know a dj, have a party. If you know a comedian, have a comedy show. The idea is to leverage relationships to make this event happen. Be creative. Don't go into debt trying to impress. People don't expect you to have it all. Only be sure that you are extremely hospitable and thoughtful in how you host your guests..

What's considered "on brand" for you?

If you don't have a brand, think about what

you want it to be. What do you want people to feel when they hear your organization's name or see your logo? Generate your event theme with that in mind.

Your event should include these elements:

Showcase the work. You can do this with an impact story, video, performance, or any creative method you determine. People want to see the impact you've made.

Share the vision. You've crafted a compelling "ask." Use it. Share how giving will impact the lives of those you serve.

A word from a supporter. Words from a person you've helped brings unquestionable credibility.

Clear giving channels. Regularly update people with the ways they can give: giving stations, Paypal, text-to-give, online, commitment cards, etc.

Opportunity for recurring giving. This may be what gets you past 10k and beyond. This is extremely important. It's an opportunity to have ongoing relationships.

Social Media presence. Your audience can be expanded using social media. Have a person dedicated to streaming a live feed from you page, or your organization's page. Test it before hand to make sure that the sound and visual quality is up to par

Audience participation. Suggest that audience members and social media viewers text message friends to invite them to the website. Advise them that if they cannot give in the moment, they can suggest a date and amount (see sample forms / communications). You can then fill out a form for them, or send an email.

*TRACKER. Have a visible tracker to show your progress throughout the event. There must be someone (or a team) dedicated to monitoring and totaling the giving receipts/amount. The tracker will keep people excited and motivated.

Establish you goal.

Budget/Itemize your needs. Share your plans with the team. Don't hold back what you are thinking. Be open to feedback. Your goal may be $10K, or it may be a different amount.

It may be tempting to go small, but be sure not to underestimate your need. Better to set the goal too high than too low. The new level that you are going to requires that you be bold and unafraid. Be honest with yourself so that you can act (and ask) with integrity and certainty.

At the start of one particular campaign, we realized that many of the things we wanted to raise money for could be (and were) donated. The financial need was now less, but the $10K value was still met. Once you get a win on this level, your competencies and expectations will increase and it'll be easier the next time.

Advertising

It doesn't take a lot of money (or any at all) to advertise. You already have effective channels to reach the people you need to reach. But you have to be intentional. (The hope is to be consistent and not annoying.)

Your advertising should be organic and not forced. Maximize the reach you already have and leverage the connections of your team. It's great to have new faces in the place, but focus more on an inside-out approach. Your team plays an important role here. If you are a part of an organization that has staff, partners, or benefactors outside of your team, they can also play a huge role in sharing your message.

Help your team invite others by asking them to and equipping them. The best advertisement at this stage is a personal invitation from you and the people connected to your cause. Provide as many people as possible with the digital flyer. Let the graphic do the work. It's never a bad move to secure professional graphic design. But there are free apps that make graphic design easy.

Here are the most effective ways to market your event at this level:

Email. Email your database 1 time weekly with the invitation.

Text Messages. Use a graphic to send invitations through text message. 1x weekly.

Social Media. Use social media to help people keep your event in the forefront of people's minds and help shape their attitude about your efforts. Post a new video invitation every day. Ask as many supporters as possible to share your posts and create regular posts of their own. This can help you determine people's perception of your event.

Calls. Calls are still king. A call communicates seriousness. It requires courage on your part and shows respect to the recipient. Some people prefer text messages. From those folks, you'll likely get a message that says, "text me. I'm in a meeting," even though they are probable watching Monday Night Football or scrolling social media. Make calls to those folks who don't mind picking up - that's the sweet spot.

Step 5
FOLLOW UP FRIDAY
systems that turn interest into investment

Put simply, development is "minding" and "mining" your relationships.

Your fundraiser isn't over yet. If you are establishing your organization, the term development is probably new to you. Fundraising is simply raising money, but development is much more important. Put simply, development is

"minding" and "mining" your relationships.

By *minding*, I mean BUILDING THE DATABASE. You do this by always capturing information, paying attention to who you know, what you know about them and recording and cataloguing it. It's being a good steward over your contacts and cultivating movement in your relationships. Everyone who was gracious enough to share anything with you, even if just an email address, needs to hear from you.

By *"mining,"* BUILDING RELATIONSHIPS FROM THE DATABASE. You do this by learning more about your network list, discerning how you can mutually benefit one another and cataloguing it. Consider a relationship management software. It's never too soon to invest in quality programs. This is what successful organizations do in the 21st century: responsibly request and collect relevant data, protect it, and build relationships through means that individuals have approved the info provided.

There are people in your database who have the capacity to do much more than they have done. Some can be available to volunteer. Some can offer expertise. Almost everyone in your database can give more than what they have. It's up to you to do your research.

The most profitable habits you can have is to email regularly (once a month) and to call. Emails are easy. Calls can be difficult. But you have to get comfortable making calls. You'll likely reach a lot of voicemail boxes, but that's okay. Have a crafted message to say hello and thank you. When you do reach someone, also be prepared to have friendly conversation and ask thoughtful questions.

Follow up can make the difference between a one-time gift or a continuous commitment. When it's done well, it can result in an increase of the size of the next gift. The quality of your follow-up is an indication of how you manage what's given.

I've learned from the follow up, or lack thereof, from the organizations I support. I take into account how I feel when I receive a thoughtful response. I also consider how I feel when I receive a short, canned message. Some organizations give a small thanks for a small gift and I take note of that to be sure that I don't do the same. What you may see as a small gift may be an intentional and sizable sacrifice from a supporter.

I support an organization that sends a canned email for every gift that I give. I don't give to hear "thank you," but I do take note of how little my gift is perceived to be. As I increase in giving to other organizations, my commitment to this particular organization will remain the same or cease altogether.

This is EVERYTHING. Your ability to do this with excellence is a foreshadowing of your long-term sustainability. This is the extra mile that most folks don't go. And, if you don't reach your goal during the event, this may be the component that pushes you over the top.

1. **The thank you to those who gave should include:**

    a. "Thank you" using preferred method of communication

    b. Amount of gift given

    c. Results of campaign

    d. Note signaling if gift is tax-deductible

    e. A call to action - visit website, social media, etc.

    f. Opportunity for recurring giving

2. **A thank you to those who came but did not give should include:**

   a. "Thank you" using preferred method of communication

   b. Results of campaign

   c. Note signaling if gift is tax-deductible

   d. A call to action - give, visit website, social media, etc.

3. **A commitment reminder should include:**

   a. Thank you using preferred method of communication

   b. Results of campaign

   c. Note signaling if gift is tax-deductible

   d. A call to action - visit website, social media, etc.

After the campaign

There was a special group of people who worked hard to help you get here.

It's normal to think about who did and who didn't support. There will undoubtedly be folks that you were counting on who didn't show up. Don't be upset at family members and friends who didn't show up, or give. It's a mistake to think that your growth and momentum depends on their support. That may not be their role in your life. Placing demands on them that they didn't agree to won't help you or your relationship with them. It's not easy being the friend, or family, of a builder/fundraiser. They owe you nothing more.

There is a special group of people who worked hard to help you get here. Show extra appreciation to your team. This is a time for you all to celebrate. Don't downplay this opportunity. Your team deserves it. And, you'll likely call on them again. But for now, the project is over and it's important that you bring closure and give them an opportunity to formally step away from the roles they assumed. A dinner, or a small gathering, are a couple of ways to bring your team together to say thank you.

TEMPLATES

Script for planning team:

I'm/Org/ is campaigning for 10K for the women in the domestic violence shelter. Would you be on the planning team? Could you join a ZOOM meeting on _____ to learn more about it?

Text and social media post script for audience participants:

I'm at Timothy's STEAM program event. They are raising money for ___. I gave ___ because they deserve it. Can you give any amount to help reach our goal by 9pm? OR pledge to give by ___? Obviously, I'm excited! We are making good progress!

Pledge cards:

Name:
Pone:
Email:
Amount pledged: by date:

ABOUT THE AUTHOR

D'Andre Ash is from Decatur, Georgia. He is married to Dr. Sheree King Ash, a practicing psychologist. Together they have a young daughter. He is a graduate of Mercer University with a bachelor's degree in organizational leadership and Columbia Theological Seminary with a master's degree in practical theology. He has a history of community leadership. In 2003 he was named an NFL Community Quarterback by NFL Charities and won a competitive grant award to fund his program, Character Builders for Young Men.

In 2008, he co-founded Gadites – a ministry helping men in transition from life in the streets to the church and on to productive lives. In 2009, he founded Extraordinary Church in Conyers, Georgia. In 2016, he founded Academy Christian Preparatory School.

He has served as a development leader for nonprofit organizations directing campaigns for causes with which he identifies.

Currently, D'Andre is called to public ministry - teaching and writing to empower individuals and organizations who seek to influence positive change for the underserved and under-resourced.

For other books and products, visit:

www.howtoraise10k.com